Look Closely

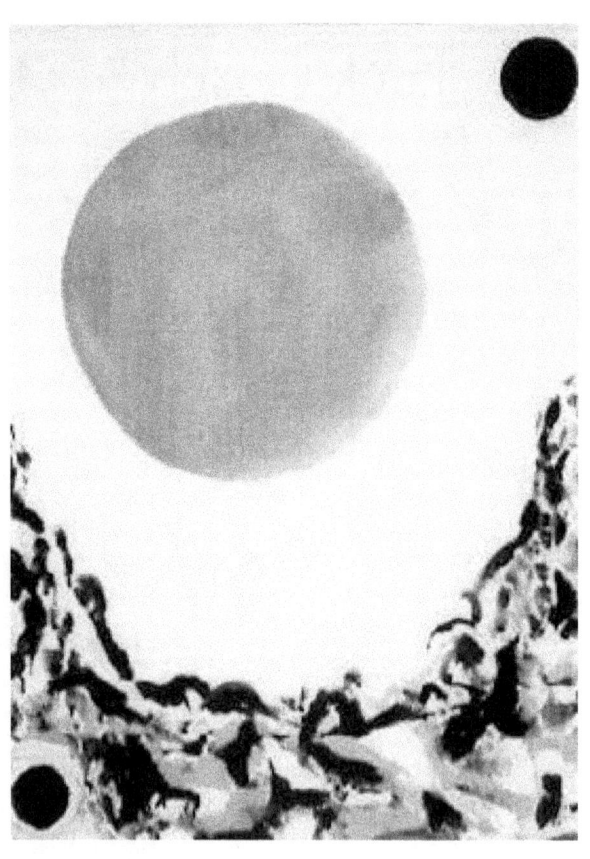

Look Closely

A Collection of Haiku

DAVID H. ROSEN

Foreword by
Shelley Baker-Gard

RESOURCE *Publications* • Eugene, Oregon

LOOK CLOSELY
A Collection of Haiku

Copyright © 2019 David H. Rosen. All rights reserved. Except for brief quotations in critical publications or reviews, no part of this book may be reproduced in any manner without prior written permission from the publisher. Write: Permissions, Wipf and Stock Publishers, 199 W. 8th Ave., Suite 3, Eugene, OR 97401.

Resource Publications
An Imprint of Wipf and Stock Publishers
199 W. 8th Ave., Suite 3
Eugene, OR 97401

www.wipfandstock.com

PAPERBACK ISBN: 978-1-5326-8792-1
HARDCOVER ISBN: 978-1-5326-8793-8
EBOOK ISBN: 978-1-5326-8793-8

Manufactured in the U.S.A.   04/26/19

Foreword

Haiku captures a moment in time that surprises or reveals a truth to the haijin (haiku poet). If the haijin composes the haiku well, its meaning is transferred to the reader who is then able to time travel to that very moment to share the experience. David H. Rosen is a widely recognized haiku master who has numerous publications to his credit. In this latest collection of his more recently composed haiku, he is asking the reader to "Look Closely," that is, to pause and imagine—those who do will be rewarded with many tiny journeys.

Shelley Baker-Gard
Portland, OR

SELECT TITLES BY DAVID H. ROSEN

Children's Books

Henry's Tower
Time, Love and Licorice: A Healing Coloring Storybook
Samantha the Sleuth & Zack's Hard Lesson
Kindergarten Symphony: An ABC Book

Poetry

The Healing Spirit of Haiku (With Joel Weishaus)
Clouds and More Clouds
Spelunking through Life: A Collection of Haiku
Living with Evergreens: A Collection of Haiku
In Search of the Hidden Pond: A Collection of Haiku
White Rose, Red Rose: A Collection of Haiku (With Johnny Baranski)
Torii Haiku: Profane to a Sacred Life

Non-Fiction

Medicine as a Human Experience (With David Reiser)
Transforming Depression: Healing the Soul through Creativity
The Tao of Jung: The Way of Integrity
The Tao of Elvis
Lost in the Long White Cloud: Finding My Way Home
Patient-Centered Medicine: A Human Experience (With Uyen Hoang)
The Alchemy of Cooking: Recipes with a Jungian Twist
Opal Whiteley's Beginning and Hoops & Hoopla

Acknowledgments

I acknowledge Bonnie Sheehey and Rebekah Sinclair for their editorial assistance. My lovely wife, Lanara, remains a permanent inspiration. Nature is an ever-present influence. As I mention in the first poem, I honor Johnny Baranski, a dear friend and a damn good poet. I thank Robert Epstein for his feedback and I deeply appreciate the foreword by Shelley Baker-Gard. Again, another excellent job by Wipf & Stock Publishers and specifically I thank James Stock, Jim Tedrick, and their staff.

My friend
suddenly died . . .
this old man is crying

(In Memory of Johnny Baranski)

Morning glory
evening glory -
same

Texas rattlesnake
shot dead
in the chili peppers

Werther effect...
damn Columbine

Spotted towhee
in the grass -
vanishes

Seed the clouds
with our love . . .
let it rain

Two solitudes
end of the lane . . .
dream come true

Look closely -
wind blown
lavender and me

Kidney stone
brought to my knees -
knife in the back

MS has ravaged me -
husk of my
former self

Everyone gets a walker . . . eventually

Doctor means teacher
It's all Greek to me

Illness, the great teacher,
new moon

Silver moon, leaving the ivory tower.

Lonely owl on a branch,
when to retire?

Existentially, it doesn't matter

37 straight losses . . . a national record
Hoops and Hoopla

Elvis, Mohammad Ali, Jesus . . .
three faces
recognized everywhere

Light in darkness, nurturing the blue

Elvis, the actor?
no, but he had soul

Elvis, the performer?
yes, everlasting

Reaching out,
a hand
finds another

Rain drops . . .
roots deepen

Creek flowing . . .
soul sounds

By the pond
in between
showers

No worries . . . knowing is overrated

Everything is nothing and my friend

Two solitudes in the forest . . . one soul

Stars
hidden by clouds . . .
homeless moon

Old man wandering
in a young night -
it doesn't matter

Old man wandering
in a young night -
wife by his side

Old man wandering
in a young night -
a knock at the door

Old man wandering
in a young night -
come in dear one

Old man wandering
in a young night -
love says "I'm here"

Everyday life . . .
red leaves falling

Cool day . . . quiet and still

Dreaming
I was a turtle . . .
that's slow

Believe it or not, I'm a sit down comic

Students need laughter to learn
professing leads to comedy

Contrary to my wife's liking,
I chose the stage name
Dr. Nada

I didn't go to med school for nothing

Feeling liberated . . .
taking that name

By the pond
all around
no sound

Across the tracks . . .
ear on rail,
the train is coming

Silence all around —
nothingness

Circling the pond
nothing to do
just be

Pitch black —
where's my grandson?

In the pond . . . the sky, where I'm headed

Tomorrow, I'll be a marigold

Once you're in the ground
it's over

Filling the pond . . .
dusk rolls in

Tall trees,
sound of wind . . .
like water

Beet leaves burst
through straw . . .
"hello strawberries"

Our place in nature,
the real culture

Green land . . . where we live and grow

Sunrise of a fairy,
Opal Whiteley

Child naturalist,
she rests in Highgate Cemetery
not far from Karl Marx

Quiet day, lovely and cool.
Yikes, fire!

Red sun . . . land of memories

Birds, flowers, gentle breeze, paradise realized

Spring mist . . .
plum blossoms

In the garden . . .
a sole robin

At least we'll
be greeted by Him & Her
on the other side

Fallen pine
over clear water . . .
sound of bird-song

Goddess of nature
upset and quakes

Be careful of the white camas

In a wild red rose lurks a bumblebee

You see me, I see you . . .
red fox

Without shadow, we are nothing

My little soul
joins the big Soul

I met
the love of my life
on a bench in New Zealand

Call it paradise, if you like

Years later, another bench . . .
frog songs, full moon

Autumn chill . . .
   chair where
grandfather died

Confucius say . . . nothing

Buddha listens . . . deeply

I saw a Zen priest
he saw me . . .
we laughed

www.ingramcontent.com/pod-product-compliance
Lightning Source LLC
Chambersburg PA
CBHW061502040426
42450CB00008B/1456